SHARING THE GOSPEL

WITH A

JEHOVAH'S WITNESS

SHARING THE GOSPEL

WITH A

JEHOVAH'S WITNESS

SHARING THE GOSPEL

WITH A
JEHOVAH'S WITNESS

TONY BROWN

10 Publishing
a division of 10ofthose.com

Copyright © 2019 by Tony Brown
First published in Great Britain in 2019

British Library Cataloguing in Publication Data
A record for this book is available from the British Library

ISBN: 978-1-912373-62-8

Designed and typeset by Pete Barnsley (CreativeHoot.com)

Printed in Denmark by Nørhaven

10Publishing, a division of 10ofthose.com
Unit C, Tomlinson Road, Leyland, PR25 2DY, England

Email: info@10ofthose.com
Website: www.10ofthose.com

CONTENTS

1

CHOOSE THIS DAY WHOM YOU WILL SERVE

Jehovah's Witnesses knock on your door, usually at an inconvenient time, and are keen to talk to you about the state of the world. Should you choose to listen to them, you will no doubt find yourself agreeing with much of what they say: 'Don't you think that the world is a scary place?' They continue, 'You know, the Bible tells us about a time when this would be the case.' Opening their Bible – a different version called the New World Translation – they read to you from Matthew 24:

You are going to hear of wars and reports of wars. See that you are not alarmed, for these things must take place, but the end is not yet. For nation will rise against nation and kingdom against kingdom, and there will be food shortages and earthquakes in one place after another. All these things are a beginning of pangs of distress (NWT, verses 6–8).

Then they explain, 'Yes, bad news is everywhere, but there is some good news. Soon, and very soon, Jehovah will rid the earth of such lawless ones, and righteousness and peace will reign on a paradise earth. Don't you long for peace and security? Wouldn't you like to live forever on a paradise earth?'

THE GOSPEL OF JEHOVAH'S WITNESSES

As a former Jehovah's Witness, I used to go 'publishing' (the term they use for door knocking). I remember being so nervous the first time, but they told me all would be well as we were going to a 'nice area of Bradford' (yes, that exists) and the people there would be polite to us. So, you can imagine my utter shock when, at the very first door, a householder launched an aggressive verbal tirade on the two sisters who knocked on the adjacent door. Fortunately, this was a rare occurrence. Most of the time we were met with one of three responses. Firstly, and most commonly, apathy: 'Thank you, but I am not interested.' Secondly, and occasionally, religion: 'Thank you, but I have my own beliefs.' Thirdly, and very occasionally, interest: 'Thank you, would you like to come in?'

What do you do when Jehovah's Witnesses knock at your door? That is what this book is about. It will hopefully encourage you to get from behind the sofa and open the door. It aims to equip you to make the most of the evangelistic opportunity on your doorstep. You can (and should) share the gospel with the Jehovah's Witnesses at your door, as the Apostle Paul instructs us: *'But how are they to call on him in whom they have not believed? And how are they to believe in him of whom they have never heard? And how are they to hear without someone preaching?'* (Romans 10:14).

2

'WE ARE JEHOVAH'S WITNESSES'

We're Jehovah's Witnesses.
We speak out in fearlessness.
Ours is the God of true prophecy;
What he foretells comes to be.

(Song 63: 'We're Jehovah's Witnesses!')

Although they call themselves Jehovah's 'Christian' Witnesses, their teachings reveal that they are far from *the faith that was once for all delivered to the saints* (Jude 1:3). Yet they consider themselves to be the only true Christian group on the face of the earth – the only group truly preaching the gospel, and the only group through whom a person can escape the 'soon-to-come' wrath of God (Armageddon): '*Only Jehovah's Witnesses*, those of the anointed remnant and the "great crowd," as a united organization under the protection of the Supreme Organizer, *have any Scriptural hope of surviving* the impending end of this doomed system dominated by Satan the Devil.'[1]

The 'united organization' mentioned is the Watch Tower Bible and Tract Society. This is the organisation that they think is under the 'protection of the Supreme Organizer' (Jehovah). It is to this organisation that every Jehovah's Witness pledges allegiance.

Jehovah's Witnesses believe that you cannot understand the Bible unless you are part of their group: 'We all need help to understand the Bible, and we cannot find the Scriptural guidance we need outside the "faithful and discreet slave" organization.'[2] They also claim that you need to be part of this organisation to have any chance of receiving eternal life: 'Similarly, Jehovah is

6

using *only one organization today* to accomplish his will. *To receive everlasting life* in the earthly Paradise we must identify that organization and serve God as part of it.'[3]

As we seek to share the gospel with Jehovah's Witnesses, it is vitally important to understand that the organisation is everything to them. It is the organisation, not the Bible, that governs the life and practice of every Jehovah's Witness. That is why, if you ever get into Bible ping-pong with them, it very rarely gets anywhere. Allegedly, you cannot understand what the Bible teaches because you are not in the 'organisation'. Therefore, they believe, however sincere a Christian you may be, you have nothing to teach them.

THE 'NOT SO' FREE HOME BIBLE STUDY

So how does a person come to believe that the Watch Tower Society is 'God's Organisation'? The Jehovah's Witnesses claim to teach only what the Bible teaches, but no matter how sincerely they believe this, it is not true. You will often hear Jehovah's Witnesses say that they researched everything for themselves, looking at lots of different Bibles and commentaries, and this led them to the 'Truth'. However, those who begin a 'Bible study' with the Jehovah's Witnesses will only ever see Watch Tower literature and only hear Watch Tower theology. If householders have no biblical knowledge, which was the case with me, then they will be led to believe that what they are being taught is what the Bible teaches. Whilst individuals can read the Bible for themselves, it's claimed that they can only understand it with the help of the Jehovah's Witnesses.

Therefore those interested in what the Jehovah's Witnesses have to say will be offered a free home Bible study, during which they can consider with some Jehovah's Witnesses what the Bible 'really' teaches. But there are a couple of things to note here. Firstly, it is not free. Beginning a study with Jehovah's Witnesses can be extremely costly. It can cost you your family, your life and your critical thinking.

This is not mere assertion. The Jehovah's Witnesses, like most religious cults, become your new family. You are taught: '"Therefore, get out from among them, and separate yourselves," says Jehovah, "and quit touching the unclean thing; and I will take you in. And I will become a father to you, and you will become sons and daughters to me," says Jehovah, the Almighty' (2 Corinthians 6:17–18, NWT). A particular favourite taught to young Jehovah's Witnesses is: 'Bad associations spoil useful habits' (1 Corinthians 15:33, NWT).

When I was a Jehovah's Witness, I remember spending all my spare time with this group and challenging my family constantly: 'Unless you become a Jehovah's Witness, you will never see our mother again.' I believed, as all Jehovah's Witnesses believe, that Armageddon was imminent. I thought that if my family continued to reject Jehovah they would be annihilated, so they urgently needed to join the organisation to be saved.[4] As a result, I was only interested in my family when they were interested in what I had to say – which wasn't very often!

Cults therefore separate you from your family unless, of course, your family is part of the group. On the other hand, to leave the Jehovah's Witnesses whilst your family remains in the group is to leave Jehovah and consequently to have your family shun you.

Secondly, though Jehovah's Witnesses offer a free home 'Bible' study, in reality they give a free home Watch Tower book study. Their aim is to take people through an organisational publication that will teach organisational theology. To be fair to the Jehovah's Witnesses knocking on your door, they do not realise this. They sincerely believe that what they are teaching is biblical truth. However, the Watch Tower book, like all their publications, is not what the Bible really teaches. Rather, it is what the Watch Tower Society teaches.

Jehovah's Witnesses believe everything that is taught in Watch Tower publications is true, but not because like the noble Bereans, they are *examining the Scriptures daily to see if these things were so'* (Acts 17:11). Rather, it is because they are captive to a concept, as former Jehovah's Witness Don Cameron explains:

> Their concept of 'the organisation' is the dominant, controlling force in their lives without them realizing it. Total belief in this concept explains why Jehovah's Witnesses are so willing to

accept whatever comes to them from the Watchtower Society no matter how complicated it is or how impossible it may be to understand, and even if it doesn't make any sense to them. They view what comes from 'God's organisation' as coming from God himself.[5]

Therefore, in the mind of the Jehovah's Witness, to leave the organisation is to leave God, and to leave God is to forfeit any chance of surviving God's impending judgment.

3

A HISTORY OF THE JEHOVAH'S WITNESSES

The founder of the Jehovah's Witnesses was a man named Charles Taze Russell, but the organisation we have today is almost unrecognisable from the group he began back in the 1870s. For a start Russell would not have been familiar with the name Jehovah's Witnesses, which was not adopted until 1931, some fifteen years after his death. The group he founded were known as the International Bible Students.

Their stated purpose was to study the Bible and to return to its original teaching. In searching through the Scriptures, Russell and his Bible students determined that churches had drifted far from biblical truth, because certain teachings long held by Christendom were false. They rejected the immortality of the soul and the traditional understanding of hell as a place of eternal torment. In their opinion nineteenth-century Christianity had lost hold of what the Bible really teaches because of the foretold apostasy of the church.

Russell was also heavily influenced by Adventist preaching, with its emphasis on the second coming of Christ. He adopted much of the chronology of the famous Adventist William Miller, who claimed that Christ would return in 1844. Though Miller was wrong, Russell believed that Miller was onto something, and he began to develop Miller's chronology for the second coming of Christ. This led to Russell teaching that Christ would return in 1874 and that all Christians who had died would be resurrected in 1878.

In 1877 Russell and a Second Adventist teacher named Nelson H. Barbour published a book entitled *Three Worlds or Plan of Redemption*.

In it, the pair claimed that Jesus did return in 1874, invisibly! They also taught that Christ's 'invisible' return triggered a forty-year harvest period that would end in 1914 with the Battle of Armageddon.

A couple of years later, in 1879, Russell started printing his own publication entitled *Zion's Watchtower and Herald of Christ's Presence*. Then, in 1881, he founded Zion's Watch Tower Tract Society. The name changed in 1896 to The Watch Tower Bible and Tract Society. Russell began to share his views in his publications, the most significant of which was his six-volume *Studies in the Scriptures*. He deviated from orthodox Biblical teaching in several ways. As mentioned before, he denied the existence of a literal hell. He also rejected the Trinity and the inherent immortality of the soul.

The Jehovah's Witnesses today teach that Russell was not the founder of a new religion, but a sincere Bible student who restored what the Bible 'really' teaches. This process has continued since the 1870s with their claim today that biblical truth can only be found in the Watch Tower organisation.

When Russell died in 1916, there was some dispute regarding the organisation and who should be the new leader. It was Joseph 'Judge' Rutherford who emerged triumphant, but this was not accepted by some loyal to Charles Russell. From this splinter groups like the International Bible Students' Association and the Russellites appeared, some of which continue to this day.

Rutherford began to change both the organisation and its doctrine. Under his leadership came many of the distinctive teachings that Jehovah's Witnesses hold today. It was Rutherford who came up with the name 'Jehovah's Witnesses', taken from Isaiah 43:10: '"You are my witnesses," declares Jehovah' (as rendered in their New World Translation of the Holy Scriptures).

When Rutherford died in 1942, he was succeeded by Nathan Homer Knorr, who was very much an organiser. It was he who launched the vast printing campaign, making Watch Tower literature widely available to the public. Through these publications the organisation grew massively. In turn Knorr was followed by Fred Franz, who was President when the much anticipated 1975 prophecy failed to materialise.

The Watch Tower Organisation, through its publications, had pointed to 1975 as a significant year. Such was the buzz of expectation that people gave up employment and sold businesses and property to spend more time door knocking. There was nothing more important than this 'field ministry' as Armageddon approached.

As 1975 came and went, many disillusioned Jehovah's Witnesses left the organisation, citing the failed prophecy as their reason. Today the organisation teaches that the mention of 1975 was only offered as a possibility and that individual members took it too far. However, their own publications from the time show that what was presented to the faithful was far from just a possibility:

Well now, as Jehovah's Witnesses, as runners, even though some of us have become a little weary, it almost seems as though Jehovah has provided meat in due season. Because he's held up before all of us, a new goal. A new year. Something to reach out for and it just seems it has given all of us so much more energy and power in this final burst of speed to the finish line. And that's the year 1975. Well, we don't have to guess what the year 1975 means if we read the Watchtower. And don't wait 'til 1975. The door is going to be shut before then. As one brother put it, 'Stay alive to Seventy-Five.'[6]

Also, in a 1980 *Watchtower* magazine, an admission was made that they did teach and believe that Christ's millennial reign would begin in 1975:

With the appearance of the book Life Everlasting – in Freedom of the Sons of God, and its comments as to how appropriate it would be for the millennial reign of Christ to parallel the seventh millennium of man's existence, considerable expectation was aroused regarding the year 1975 ... Unfortunately, however, along with such cautionary information, there were other statements published that implied that such realization of hopes by that year was more of a probability than a mere possibility.[7]

In 1976 control of what was taught and published shifted from the President of the Watch Tower Bible and Tract Society to a group called the Governing Body. This meant that the Society's Presidents had significantly less power. When Franz passed away in 1992, Milton Henschel became President until 2000. Since then, Presidents have been no more than figureheads and are considered assistants to the Governing Body.

You may think that this move from a single leader to group leadership sounds like a positive safeguard. Sadly this is not the case because power has just shifted from a single man who spoke for God to a group of men that now speak for God. The Governing Body operate from the World Headquarters of Jehovah's Witnesses in Warwick, New York. They are believed to be 'the faithful and discreet slave, who give out food at the proper time' (see Matthew 24:45). They alone are believed to speak for Jehovah.

4

WHY BECOME A JEHOVAH'S WITNESS?

Why do people join the Jehovah's Witnesses? Do people join the Jehovah's Witnesses? These may appear contradictory questions, but they are not. Most, if not all, cult members believe they freely joined the group. It was their choice to join and, should they choose to, it is their choice to leave. But this is sadly often not the case.

People don't join cults; people are recruited into cults. Many who 'join' the Jehovah's Witnesses may have had a reason for beginning a 'Bible' study with them. Perhaps they were recently bereaved, lonely, spiritually curious, disillusioned with life, or so on. In fact, they didn't join the group because of these things, but rather because they were recruited by a methodology.

At the time of writing, the main recruiting tool of the Jehovah's Witnesses is their book *What Does the Bible Really Teach?* Like all its predecessors, it systematically teaches the interested person Watch Tower doctrine. Each chapter is split into sections where a paragraph is read and then a question asked. The answer to that question is always found in the body of the paragraph, so you just repeat what you have read. As the chapters are 'sprinkled' with Bible verses, individuals believe they are being taught what the Bible really teaches. In reality, they are being indoctrinated with Watch Tower theology.

This very simple, almost childlike, way of teaching is incredibly effective. Within weeks the unsuspecting inquirer is beginning to develop a Watch Tower 'mind' which takes on board, and believes, all that it is told. Slowly, the group becomes your family and the Watch Tower mission becomes your life. It doesn't take long before you are dressing, walking and talking like a Jehovah's Witness. Instead of enjoying the much-appreciated Saturday lie in, you are waking others by knocking on their doors.

How then do we reach one who is thoroughly convinced they have found the 'truth'? In the following chapters we will look at some of the core beliefs of Jehovah's Witnesses and consider how we may respond to them.

5

THE NAME 'JEHOVAH'

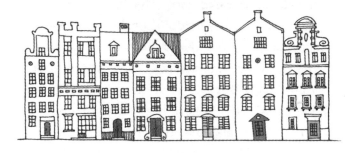

Jehovah's Witness teaching:
'"You are my witnesses," declares
Jehovah' (NWT).

As mentioned in chapter three, the Jehovah's Witnesses take their name from their own translation (the New World Translation) of Isaiah 43:10. This replaces the word 'LORD' in the Old Testament with the name 'Jehovah', which is of utmost important to the Jehovah's Witness.

As they are told that Jehovah is God's name and must be used, it is no surprise that this topic is addressed very early on in their recruiting manual.

The Jehovah's Witnesses ask, 'What is the truth about God? Does God have a name?' The unsuspecting student is then surprised when the Jehovah's Witnesses show that the Authorised Bible (King James Version) uses the divine name: *'that men may know that thou, whose name alone is Jehovah, art the most high over all the earth'* (Psalm 83:18). But this is not the practice of most Bible translators. Where the Hebrew name for God 'YHWH' appears, they translate it 'Lord' for a couple of reasons.

Firstly, the Jews developed a practice of not using the name for fear of mispronouncing it. As written Hebrew had only consonants and no vowels, they were concerned to not take the name of God in vain (Exodus 20:7). So they replaced 'YHWH' with the Hebrew word *Adonai* ('Lord'). Secondly, as the translators themselves are unsure how the name should be rendered, they follow suit and use the word 'Lord'.

THE ORIGIN OF THE NAME 'JEHOVAH'

The Hebrew letters 'YHWH' was transliterated into Latin to become 'JHVH'. The next question facing the Bible translators was which vowels should be placed in 'JHVH' to make it pronounceable. Should it be the vowels from *Adonai*, *Elohim* (another Hebrew name for God) or some other word? Christian scholars in the thirteenth century decided to add vowels from *Adonai* to the letters 'JHVH' and so created the name 'JaHoVaH'. This fact is verified by the Watch Tower in its publication *Aid to Bible Understanding*, where it says that the name 'Jehovah' was first written by a Spanish Dominican Monk named Raymundus Martini in 1270 AD.[8] However, the Jehovah's Witnesses are insistent that the correct pronunciation of God's name is 'Jehovah', though they have admitted themselves, along with the overwhelming consensus of scholars, that the most accurate rendering of 'YHWH' should be 'Yahweh'.

TIP:

When told that we cannot possibly know the correct way to pronounce YHWH,

CONTINUE ↓

because we don't know which vowels to add in, the Jehovah's Witnesses may say that God will be happy that they are at least trying to get his name right. Ask them why he would be happy if they were mispronouncing his name.

To prove your point to a Jehovah's Witness, try replacing the vowels in their name with alternatives so that you call them something else. How do they feel about this? For example, if you replaced the 'o' in my name with 'i', renaming me 'Tiny', then I wouldn't be happy as that is not my name!

THE IMPORTANCE OF GOD'S NAME

Even then the issue is not so much that the Witnesses use the name 'Jehovah' and are adamant on this pronunciation. The key problem lies in their insistence that this name must be used to honour God.

Jehovah's Witnesses will point out what Jesus himself said about God's name: *'I made known to them your name, and I will continue to make it known, that the love with which you have loved me may be in them, and I in them'* (John 17:26). Then they will ask, 'If Jesus said that God has a name, and he made it known to people, doesn't it follow that he used that name and we should too?' This seems like a reasonable assumption, until we investigate what name Jesus did make known to the people. Jesus is never recorded using the name 'Jehovah' ('YHWH'). In fact, that name is not found in the Greek New Testament. Rather the word *Kurios* (Greek for 'Lord') is used.

Furthermore, name, in the sense of John 17:26, is all to do with reputation and not pronunciation. If we say that a person has a 'good name', we are not talking about the person's Christian name: Fred, Jack or even Tony. We are talking about a person's character. In the same way Jesus revealed God's character: *'No longer do I call you servants, for the servant does not know what his master is doing; but I have called you friends, for all that I have heard from my Father I have made known to you'* (John 15:15).

The Watch Tower publication *What Does the Bible Really Teach?* asks these questions: 'If you want someone to get to know you, what might you do? Would you not tell the person your name? Does God have a name?' The final part of a Christian's answer to this argument is that God does indeed have a name, which Jesus revealed repeatedly to his followers. That name is 'Father'. How wonderful is that name? We can call the Creator God 'Father'. What's more, as we address him as 'Father', we are aware that we are his sons and daughters. What a joy and privilege to know God as Father.

QUESTIONS FOR JEHOVAH'S WITNESSES

- Acts 1:8 says, *'But you will receive power when the Holy Spirit has come upon you, and you will be my witnesses in Jerusalem and in all Judea and Samaria, and to the end of the earth.'* So, whose witnesses are we to be?

- Philippians 2:9–11 reads, *'Therefore God has highly exalted him and bestowed on him the name that is above every name, so that at the name of Jesus every knee should bow,*

CONTINUE ➡

in heaven and on earth and under the earth, and every tongue confess that Jesus Christ is Lord, to the glory of God the Father.' So according to the Bible, who has the highest name?

• Acts 2:21 says, 'And it shall come to pass that everyone who calls upon the name of the Lord shall be saved.' Acts 4:12 reads, 'And there is salvation in no one else, for there is no other name under heaven given among men by which we must be saved.' So, by which name are we saved?

6
JESUS

Jehovah's Witness teaching:
'Jesus is Jehovah's most precious Son—
and for good reason. He is called "the
firstborn of all creation," for he was God's
first creation. (Colossians 1:15) There is
something else that makes this Son special.
He is the "only-begotten Son." (John 3:16)
This means that Jesus is the only one
directly created by God. Jesus is also
the only one whom God used when He
created all other things. (Colossians 1:16)'⁹

The 'Jesus' of the Jehovah's Witnesses is very
different to the Jesus that has been believed

upon and taught by historic, orthodox, biblical Christianity for the last 2,000 years. For Jehovah's Witnesses, Jesus is little more than a 'bit part' in Jehovah's grand plan to restore the earth to an Eden-like state.

Rather than believing Jesus to be a Saviour, Jehovah's Witnesses view him as just an example to follow. Rather than acknowledging Jesus as the eternal Son of God, he is considered a created being. Rather than recognising Jesus as God incarnate, he is seen as the archangel Michael.

Jehovah's Witnesses have their proof texts to show that Jesus isn't God. Here are a couple of examples:

You heard that I said to you, 'I am going away and I am coming back to you.' If you loved me, you would rejoice that I am going to the Father, for the Father is greater than I am (John 14:28, NWT).

He is the image of the invisible God, the first-born of all creation (Colossians 1:15, NWT).

How are we to handle such verses used by the Jehovah's Witnesses? Here are some general points to note. Firstly, it is important to always read verses given by Jehovah's Witnesses in context. The context will often give you the answer, whilst any verses lifted out of their context can be misused, misapplied and misunderstood. Secondly, be aware that many verses in their Bible, the New World Translation (NWT), have been altered, so check the verse in your own Bible. Thirdly, remember that they read Scripture through 'Watch Tower glasses'. Therefore, because they have been told that Jesus is not God, they only see verses that they believe support this view, whilst dismissing those that clearly affirm his deity. Fourthly, and importantly, if you cannot answer their so-called 'proof texts', don't think they are correct in their assertions. Don't be fooled. If you cannot answer, it doesn't mean there isn't an answer!

But what of the verses above? How do we respond to those?

JESUS' DIVINITY

The first proof text I mentioned that the Jehovah's Witnesses use is: 'You heard that I said to you, "I am going away and I am coming back to you." If you loved me, you would rejoice that I am going to the Father, for the Father is greater than I am' (John 14:28, NWT). Because the Jehovah's Witnesses deny the Trinity, they fail to see and/or acknowledge the eternal relationship between the Father and the Son.

Yet whilst on earth, Jesus never ceased being God, *'though he was in the form of God, did not count equality with God a thing to be grasped'* (Philippians 2:6).When the eternal Son of God, Jesus, came to the earth, he *'made himself nothing, taking the form of a servant, being born in the likeness of men'* (Philippians 2:7). This helps us to understand what Jesus was saying when he said, in John 14:28, *'the Father is greater than I'*. The Father remained in the Father 'position', whilst Jesus left his position alongside the Father to take on human likeness, thus lessening himself. The book of Hebrews tells us that Jesus *'for a little while was made lower than the angels'* (Hebrews 2:9). Understanding that the Father, who remains in heaven, is in a greater position than the Son, whilst he is upon the earth, helps us to deal with other verses that the Jehovah's Witnesses try to use against the deity of Christ.

TIP:

It is good to use illustrations from everyday life to help Jehovah's Witnesses understand what Scripture is teaching. You could ask them if the Queen of England is greater than they are. The answer is yes according to her position and authority (we are her subjects), but the answer is no according to her nature (we are all human beings). In the same way, the Father is greater than Jesus because of the Father's position and authority, but the Father is not greater than the Son according to their nature (they are both God).

JESUS' PRE-EMINENCE

Another favourite text of the Jehovah's Witnesses to deny the deity of Christ is: 'He is the image of the invisible God, the firstborn of all creation' (Colossians 1:15, NWT). But when Jehovah's Witnesses use this verse, you often find them quoting only part of it so that they say of Jesus, 'He is … the firstborn of all creation'. As this is a verse the Jehovah's Witnesses take completely out of context, we must impress upon them exactly what Paul is saying here. Jesus being the image of the invisible God is important information for all that follows. Here is the relevant verse in its context, and according to the accurate ESV translation:

He is the image of the invisible God, the firstborn of all creation. For by him all things were created, in heaven and on earth, visible and invisible, whether thrones or dominions or rulers or authorities—all things were created through him and for him. And he is before all things, and in him all things hold together. And he is the head of the body, the church. He is the beginning, the firstborn from the dead, that in everything he might be pre-eminent. For in him all the fullness of God was pleased to dwell, and through him

*to reconcile to himself all things, whether on
earth or in heaven, making peace by the blood
of his cross (Colossians 1:15–20).*

Compare this with the New World Translation
of the same passage:

He is the image of the invisible God, the
firstborn of all creation; because by means
of him all *other* things were created in the
heavens and on the earth, the things visible
and the things invisible, whether they
are thrones or lordships or governments
or authorities. All *other* things have been
created through him and for him. Also,
he is before all *other* things, and by means
of him all *other* things were made to
exist, and he is the head of the body, the
congregation. He is the beginning, the
firstborn from the dead, so that he might
become the one who is first in all things;
because God was pleased to have all
fullness to dwell in him, and through him
to reconcile to himself all *other* things by
making peace through the blood he shed

on the torture stake, whether the things
on the earth or the things in the heavens
(NWT, italics mine).

Did you spot the difference? The New World
Translation has added the word 'other' five times
into those verses.

When challenged about this, the Jehovah's
Witnesses may try to dazzle you by referring to
the original Greek, but don't be fooled. The Greek
word *allos* meaning 'other' is not in the Greek
text, nor is there any justification for its addition.
In fact, it is important to understand that whilst
many Jehovah's Witnesses will refer to the Greek,
or Hebrew, and sound very knowledgeable about
these languages, the vast majority will only be
repeating what they have been told. They will
have never checked it out for themselves, nor are
they proficient in these languages, so don't let
them intimidate you with their references.

Furthermore, whilst the Jehovah's Witnesses
may claim that the addition of the word 'other'
does not change the text's meaning, it clearly
does. The New World Translation adds the word
'other' to obscure the deity of Christ that is

clearly revealed in these verses. Paul's statement in verse 15 sets up all that follows: Jesus is the pre-eminent one over *all* things.

TIP:

To help a Jehovah's Witness understand this point, ask them to imagine that you've been given a contract of work which said you will be paid £500 if you work every day this week. If you amended it to say that you will be paid £500 if you work every *other* day this week, have you changed the original meaning?

Jehovah's Witnesses have been taught by the Watch Tower that the phrase 'firstborn of all creation' means that Jesus was the first one to be created by Jehovah, and then Jesus created everything else. However, this is errant theology because the context shows something very different. Whilst in Scripture the word 'firstborn' can mean literally the first child to be born in a family, it can have a different meaning of being first in rank or pre-eminent.

To take another example, we find God saying of David, *'And I will make him the firstborn, the highest of the kings of the earth'* (Psalm 89:27). What does God mean here by 'firstborn'? David was not the first to be born in his family. In fact, he was the last son of Jesse. So 'firstborn' in this context must mean something different. It denotes that David is first in rank or the pre-eminent one, as the rest of the verse makes clear: he is 'the highest of the kings of the earth'.

If we replace the word 'firstborn' in Colossians 1:15 and use 'pre-eminent' in its place, all that Paul says in the following verses makes sense. Jesus is the pre-eminent one over creation because: *'by him all things were created … all things were created through him and for him … he is before all things … he is the head of the body, the church …'*

JESUS AND THE ARCHANGEL MICHAEL

A final thing to be aware of is that Jehovah's Witnesses also believe that Jesus is also the archangel Michael. There has been much discussion in the past about the identity of the archangel Michael (the name Michael means 'who is like God'), and the Watch Tower Organisation are quick to quote those – particularly 'Trinitarian' scholars – who have contended that Jesus and Michael may be one and the same. But, as always, the Watch Tower either misquotes, quotes out of context or plainly misunderstands what is being said. In technical terms verses are eisegeted (with beliefs read into the text) rather than exegeted (with beliefs being drawn out of the text).

So the Watch Tower rendering of 1 Thessalonians 4:15–16 is:

> For this is what we tell you by Jehovah's word, that we the living who survive to the presence of the Lord will in no way precede those who have fallen asleep in death; because the Lord himself will descend from heaven with a commanding call, with an archangel's+ voice and with God's trumpet, and those who are dead in union with Christ will rise first (NWT).

Note that these verses are clearly not saying that Jesus is Michael. But in the mind of a Jehovah's

Witness these verses do clearly teach that Jesus is Michael. How is that so? Their basis for this belief is because the Lord descends from heaven 'with an archangel's voice'. However, we can follow this same logic and take it to a place where the Watch Tower does not want to go. If Jesus is the archangel Michael because he descends from heaven 'with an archangel's voice', then surely it follows that he must be God because he also descends from heaven 'with God's trumpet'.

You will notice that after the word 'archangel's' in the New World Translation verses above there appears a '+' symbol. When this is clicked upon online it takes the reader to Jude 1:9: 'But when Mi'chael the archangel had a difference with the Devil and was disputing about Moses' body, he did not dare to bring a judgment against him in abusive terms, but said: "May Jehovah rebuke you"' (NWT). The Watch Tower links here to Jude 1:9 because that verse also speaks of Michael the archangel. However, this verse works against their belief that Jesus and Michael are the same being. This verse shows Michael unwilling to challenge the devil and instead calls upon Jehovah to rebuke him. But Jesus had no problem rebuking the devil and the demons, as we see from the following verses:

> Then Jesus said to him, 'Be gone, Satan! For it is written, "You shall worship the Lord your God and him only shall you serve"' (Matthew 4:10).

> But he turned and said to Peter, 'Get behind me, Satan! You are a hindrance to me. For you are not setting your mind on the things of God, but on the things of man' (Matthew 16:23).

> And Jesus rebuked him, and the demon came out of him, and the boy was healed instantly (Matthew 17:18).

The writer to the Hebrews specifically tells us that Jesus is not an angel:

> For to which of the angels did God ever say,
> 'You are my Son, today I have begotten you'?
>   Or again, 'I will be to him a father, and he shall be to me a son'?
>   And again, when he brings the firstborn

into the world, he says, 'Let all God's angels worship him.'

Of the angels he says, 'He makes his angels winds, and his ministers a flame of fire.'
But of the Son he says, 'Your throne, O God, is forever and ever, the sceptre of uprightness is the sceptre of your kingdom'
(Hebrews 1:5–8).

These verses, though, have been significantly distorted in the NWT. This is perhaps not surprising given their theology. Jehovah's Witnesses believe that Jehovah created an archangel (Michael) to be his only-begotten Son, after which Michael created everything else. Michael went out of existence when the man Jesus was born to Mary. After his death, the man Jesus disappeared, to be replaced by the newly resurrected 'Michael'. It's Michael (not Jesus) who now resides in heaven with Jehovah. Yikes! Yet there is not a single verse of Scripture that supports the notion that Jesus is the archangel Michael. In fact, Hebrews 13:8 is very clear that: *'Jesus Christ is the same yesterday and today and for ever.'*

QUESTIONS FOR JEHOVAH'S WITNESSES

- If Jehovah created Michael (Jesus) and then Michael (Jesus) created all other things, did Michael (Jesus) create Satan?

- If Jesus is also the archangel Michael and he created the angel Lucifer, does that mean they are angelic brothers?

- Who died for your sins? If Jesus and Michael are one and the same, did an angel die for your sin? How can an angel atone for sin?

- In John 5:22–23 Jesus says, *'The Father judges no one, but has given all judgment to the Son, that all may honour the Son, just as they honour the Father. Whoever does not honour the Son does not honour the Father who sent him.'* Can a created being make such a statement? Should we honour the created just as we honour the Father?

Then point them to who Jesus really is according to the Bible by looking at these verses:

CONTINUE ⬇

In the beginning was the Word, and the Word was with God, and the Word was God (John 1:1).

Thomas answered him, 'My Lord and my God!' (John 20:28).

For in him the whole fullness of deity dwells bodily (Colossians 2:9).

He is the radiance of the glory of God and the exact imprint of his nature, and he upholds the universe by the word of his power (Hebrews 1:3).

But of the Son he says, 'Your throne, O God, is for ever and ever, the sceptre of uprightness is the sceptre of your kingdom' (Hebrews 1:8).

To them belong the patriarchs, and from their race, according to the flesh, is the Christ who is God over all, blessed for ever. Amen (Romans 9:5).

… waiting for our blessed hope, the appearing of the glory of our great God and Saviour Jesus Christ (Titus 2:13).

Simon Peter, a servant and apostle of Jesus Christ, to those who have obtained a faith of

CONTINUE →

equal standing with ours by the righteousness of our God and Saviour Jesus Christ (2 Peter 1:1).

For to us a child is born, to us a son is given; and the government shall be upon his shoulder, and his name shall be called Wonderful Counsellor, Mighty God, Everlasting Father, Prince of Peace (Isaiah 9:6).

7

THE HOLY SPIRIT

Jehovah's Witness teaching:
'What is the holy spirit? ... The holy
spirit is God's power in action, his active
force. (Micah 3:8; Luke 1:35) God sends
out his spirit by projecting his energy
to any place to accomplish his will.—
Psalm 104:30; 139:7.[10]

Notice the question asks, 'What is the holy
spirit?' instead of 'Who is the holy spirit?' In the
New World Translation 'holy spirit' is also always
written in the lower case. Jehovah's Witnesses
are taught that the holy spirit is nothing more
than God's power. This 'holy spirit' is likened to
electricity flowing from God to achieve his will.

THE PERSON OF THE HOLY SPIRIT

The Bible clearly shows that the Holy Spirit is not just a mere impersonal force. Rather he has personality. He possesses a mind, emotions and a will. We see this is the following Bible verses:

For the Spirit searches everything, even the depths of God (1 Corinthians 2:10).

And do not grieve the Holy Spirit of God, by whom you were sealed for the day of redemption (Ephesians 4:30).

Likewise the Spirit helps us in our weakness. For we do not know what to pray for as we ought, but the Spirit himself intercedes for us with groanings too deep for words. And he who searches hearts knows what is the mind of the Spirit, because the Spirit intercedes for the saints according to the will of God (Romans 8:26–27).

To each is given the manifestation of the Spirit for the common good. To one is given through the Spirit the utterance of wisdom, and to another the utterance of knowledge according to the same Spirit, to another faith by the same Spirit, to another gifts of healing by the one Spirit, to another the working of miracles, to another prophecy, to another the ability to distinguish between spirits, to another various kinds of tongues, to another the interpretation of tongues. All these are empowered by one and the same Spirit who apportions to each one individually as he wills (1 Corinthians 12:7-11).

And I will ask the Father, and he will give you another Helper, to be with you for ever, even the Spirit of truth, whom the world cannot receive, because it neither sees him nor knows him. You know him for he dwells with you and will be in you (John 14:16–17).

But the Helper, the Holy Spirit, whom the Father will send in my name, he will teach you all things and bring to your remembrance all that I have said to you (John 14:26).

But when the Helper comes, whom I will send to you from the Father, the Spirit of truth, who proceeds from the Father, he will bear witness about me (John 15:26).

In contrast, being taught by the Watch Tower that the Holy Spirit is only an impersonal force leads the Jehovah's Witnesses to conclude that they have no real need of him. Demoting the Holy Spirit, and Jesus, to bit-part players strengthens their conviction that they need to seek out and worship only their unitarian God 'Jehovah'.

TIP:

Since the Watch Tower liken the Holy Spirit to electricity, suggest a Jehovah's Witness replaces references to the 'Spirit' with the word 'electricity' in the verses above. It doesn't make sense, does it? In fact, you could say it is 'shocking'!

QUESTIONS FOR JEHOVAH'S WITNESSES

- Ask them to read out Acts 13:1–2: 'Now in Antioch there were prophets and teachers in the local congregation: Bar'na·bas, Sym'e·on who was called Ni'ger, Lucius of Cy·re'ne, Man'a·en who was educated with Herod the district ruler, and Saul. As they were ministering to Jehovah and fasting, the holy spirit said,: "Set aside for me Bar'na·bas and Saul for the work to which I have called them."' Then ask them to explain to you how an electrical force, an energy from God, can say 'Set apart for *me* Barnabas and Saul for the work to which *I have called them.*'

- Also ask them to read out Acts 5:1–5 concerning the story of Ananias and Sapphira. 'However, a man named An·a·ni'as, together with his wife Sap·phi'ra, sold some property. But he secretly held back some of the price, with his wife's knowledge, and he brought just a part of it and deposited it at the feet of

CONTINUE ⬇

the apostles. But Peter said: "An·a·ni'as, why has Satan emboldened you to lie to the holy spirit and secretly hold back some of the price of the field? As long as it remained with you, did it not remain yours? And after it was sold, was it not in your control? Why have you thought up such a deed as this in your heart? You have lied, not to men, but to God." On hearing these words, An·a·ni'as collapsed and died. And great fear came over all those who heard about it' (NWT). Next ask them who, according to verse 3, Peter says that they lied to. The answer is the Holy Spirit (not to an electrical force). Then ask them to whom did Peter say they lied in verse 4. The answer is God. According to these verses the Holy Spirit and God are one and the same.

8
THE TRINITY

Jehovah's Witness teaching:
'Many Christian denominations teach
that God is a Trinity. However, note
what the Encyclopædia Britannica
states: "Neither the word Trinity nor
the explicit doctrine appears in the New
Testament ... The doctrine developed
gradually over several centuries and
through many controversies." In fact,
the God of the Bible is never described
as being part of a Trinity.'[11]

'The impression could arise that the Trinitarian dogma is in the last analysis a late 4th-century invention. In a sense, this is true ... The formulation "one God in three Persons" was not solidly established, certainly not fully assimilated into Christian life and its profession of faith, prior to the end of the 4th century.'[12]

'The Council of Nicaea met on May 20, 325 [C.E.]. Constantine himself presided, actively guiding the discussions, and personally proposed ... the crucial formula expressing the relation of Christ to God in the creed issued by the council, "of one substance with the Father." ... Overawed by the emperor, the bishops, with two exceptions only, signed the creed, many of them much against their inclination.'[13]

THE WORD 'TRINITY' AND THE BIBLE

To a Jehovah's Witness, the word 'Trinity' is like a red rag to a bull. Their opening response is usually: 'Well, you know the word "trinity" is not in the Bible, don't you?'

This, for the uninformed Christian, is often enough to put them on the back foot. From there, the Jehovah's Witness will pummel the Christian with Bible verses that appear to show that Jesus is not God.

However, the fact that the word 'Trinity' is not in the Bible is not as big an issue as they claim. In fact, the Jehovah's Witnesses themselves use 'unbiblical' words to describe biblical concepts found in the Bible. For example, they use the word 'theocratic' to describe God's rule; this word is also not in the Bible, but is perfectly acceptable to them.

There are a couple of other things we should note about their arguments, such as those quoted above. Firstly, they quote from 'Christendom's' literature to support their position. This is interesting because they tell their adherents not to read anything other than Watch Tower literature.

Secondly, when you read quotes in Watch Tower publications, you should always look out for their use of ellipses (the three dots indicating an intentional omission of words). They have a bad habit of partially quoting sources, removing the words they don't want Jehovah's Witnesses to see with a '…'

Of course, in some situations it may be that the information or thought you want to share is contained in a rather lengthy passage, so you pick out the bits you want to share, leaving out the superfluous words indicated by the three dots. That use of the ellipsis is acceptable if it does not in any way change the context or the meaning of what is being said. But Watch Tower publications use them to deliberately mislead their adherents. When you look up the extracts they quote and read them fully, you find that they often agree with an orthodox biblical view of the Trinity, rather than what the Watch Tower makes them to appear to say. This is incredibly deceptive.

TIP:

When discussing the Trinity with Jehovah's Witnesses, make sure you have control. They are programmed to teach, so they want you to listen. But on this topic have them agree to the following ground rule: that they will allow you to share why you believe the

CONTINUE →

Trinity is biblical, and then you will allow them time to respond. This is important as they will have all their anti-trinitarian proof texts ready to fire at you. It will also allow you to take the sting out of some of the verses they want to share with you, because you will use them before they do.

THE DOCTRINE OF THE TRINITY

If you asked a Jehovah's Witness to explain what they think we believe the Trinity to be, you may be surprised by their answer. Sometimes they do not understand what we mean at all. They may say, 'You believe in three Gods' or even 'a three-headed God'. Therefore we must explain the Trinity doctrine in a clear, concise way. The Trinity doctrine is the biblical belief that there is *one God*, but that *one God* is revealed in Scripture to exist in *three persons*. So God is one *what* and three *whos*.

ESTABLISHING THERE IS ONLY ONE TRUE GOD

We can establish with them that there is only *one true God* by pointing them to John 17:3.

(At this they will smile because this is one of their proof texts.) John 17:3, even in their Bible, reads: 'This means everlasting life, their coming to know you, the only true God, and the one whom you sent, Jesus Christ' (NWT). So, if we then ask, 'According to John 17:3, how many true Gods exist?' the answer is obvious: one.

Next, we can further prove this by asking them to read 2 Corinthians 4:4, again from their Bible: '... among whom the god of this system of things has blinded the minds of the unbelievers, so that the illumination of the glorious good news about the Christ, who is the image of God, might not shine through' (NWT). In that verse Satan is called the god of this world, whilst John 17:3 says that there is only one true God. From this we can ask, 'Is it right to say that Satan is a false god?'

They should agree to this, but, if necessary, persist until they agree. If there is only one true God, which the Bible clearly declares, Satan must thereby be false. This acknowledges the category of a 'false god' – as well as a true God. Furthermore, by implication all other gods named in the Bible must therefore be false. Try to get the Jehovah's Witnesses to affirm this.

The last step is to challenge them about how many Gods they believe in. This can be done by asking them to read Isaiah 9:6 in their Bible: 'For a child has been born to us, A son has been given to us; And the rulership will rest on his shoulder. His name will be called Wonderful Counselor, Mighty God, Eternal Father, Prince of Peace' (NWT). There Jesus is called a 'Mighty God'. Ask, 'If there is only one true God, is Jesus this God?' They will obviously say, 'No.' Continue, 'So is Jesus therefore a false God?' Again they will obviously say, 'No.' But as we have already established that there is only one true God and the rest are false, Jesus has to be either rightly acknowledged as this one true God or categorised as a false god. There are no other options.

This puts Jehovah's Witnesses in a difficult place. They can't say that Jesus is a true God, but neither can they say he is a false god. This leads them to create another 'unbiblical' category that allows them the notion that Jesus was somehow 'divine' but not God. They say that Jesus is Mighty

God, but not Almighty God. They consider Jesus a 'lesser god' that is neither true nor false! I once heard the story of how a confused Jehovah's Witness, upon being asked how many Gods he believed in, said: 'One and a half.' This is funny, but also very sad.

QUESTIONS FOR JEHOVAH'S WITNESSES

- Ask then to read Galatians 1:1 in their Bibles: 'Paul, an apostle, neither from men nor through a man, but through Jesus Christ and God the Father, who raised him up from the dead' (NWT). Then ask them who, according to this verse, raised Jesus from the dead. The answer is God the Father.

- Ask them now to read, John 2:15–21 about Jesus clearing the temple. Then ask them who, according to Jesus, will raise him from the dead. The answer is Jesus said he would raise himself: 'Jesus replied to them: "Tear down this temple, and in three days I will raise it up" … he was

CONTINUE ➡

talking about the temple of his body' (John 2: 19, 21, NWT). They will dispute this, but hold them to the words of Jesus. Did Jesus lie?

- Ask them next to read Romans 8:11: 'If, now, the spirit of him who raised up Jesus from the dead dwells in you, the one who raised up Christ Jesus from the dead will also make your mortal bodies alive through his spirit that resides in you.' (NWT). Then ask them who, according to this verse, raised Jesus from the dead. The answer is the Spirit. They will say 'the Spirit of him' means Jehovah, but state that the Spirit is the Holy Spirit. Finally, ask them how many times Jesus rose from the dead. Scripture shows that Jesus rose from the dead once and that the Trinity – Father, Son and Holy Spirit – were all involved.

For a list of more verses that explain the Trinity, see www.esv.org/resources/esv-global-study-bible/chart_43_10

9

SALVATION

Jehovah's Witness teaching:
'The terms "save" and "salvation" are
sometimes used by Bible writers to convey
the idea of a person's being delivered
from danger or destruction. (Exodus
14:13, 14; Acts 27:20) Often, though,
these terms refer to deliverance from sin.
(Matthew 1:21) Since death is caused by
sin, people who are saved from sin have
the hope of living forever.—John 3:16, 17.

To gain salvation, you must exercise faith
in Jesus and demonstrate that faith by

> obeying his commands.—Acts 4:10, 12;
> Romans 10:9, 10; Hebrews 5:9.

> The Bible shows that you must have
> works, or acts of obedience, to prove
> that your faith is alive. (James 2:24, 26)
> However, this does not mean that you
> can earn salvation. It is "God's gift" based
> on his "undeserved kindness," or "grace."
> —Ephesians 2:8, 9; King James Version.[14]

At first glance, the quotes above seem reasonable enough. We don't disagree that faith should lead to works, but for the Jehovah's Witness these must go together to 'prove' a person is *worthy* of eternal life. Also, notice the phrase 'exercise faith'. The addition of the word 'exercise' in their Bible and connecting it with the word 'faith' is totally unjustified, but reveals their determination to show their adherents that faith must be acted upon to have any hope of salvation. Here are some quotes from *The Watchtower*:

> Remember, though, that you must work
> hard to receive these blessings, it will cost

you time and effort ... We therefore urge one and all to lay hold on God's promises and trust him fully. By continued diligent study of the Bible and by application of its wise counsel you may attain to the grandest of blessings, including everlasting life in a paradise earth![15]

Salvation cannot be earned by attendance at meetings or in any other way. It is free, a gift from God. Yet, Jehovah God does require efforts on our part if we are to receive his gift of everlasting life.[16]

Yet sometimes faith requires nothing but trust. Compare the Jehovah's Witness view of faith with that of the Apostle Paul:

For by grace you have been saved through faith. And this is not your own doing; it is the gift of God, not a result of works, *so that no one may boast. For we are his workmanship, created in Christ Jesus for good works, which God prepared beforehand, that we should walk in them* (Ephesians 2:8–10, emphasis mine).

Paul clearly shows that salvation is not about our works; it is not about our efforts. It requires nothing but trusting in Jesus. He uses Abraham as an example of this in writing to the Romans:

> *What then shall we say was gained by Abraham, our forefather according to the flesh? For if Abraham was justified by works, he has something to boast about, but not before God. For what does the Scripture say?* 'Abraham believed God, and it was counted to him as righteousness.' *Now to the one who works, his wages are not counted as a gift but as his due. And to the one who does not work but trusts him who justifies the ungodly, his faith is counted as righteousness, just as David also speaks of the blessing of the one to whom God counts righteousness apart from works:*
>
> *'Blessed are those whose lawless deeds are forgiven,*
> *and whose sins are covered;*
> *blessed is the man against whom the Lord will not count his sin'·*
> *(Romans 4:1–8, emphasis mine).*

Notice it was Abraham's belief (faith) in God that made him righteous. Yes, he acted upon that faith, but it was 'faith alone' that justified him. As Martin Luther is claimed to have said, 'We are saved by faith alone, but the faith that saves is never alone.'

JAMES, PAUL AND FAITH

It may appear when talking to a Jehovah's Witness about salvation that we are just splitting hairs, but don't be fooled. There is an eternal difference between our positions and so it is one that needs to be addressed.

Jehovah's Witnesses support their view by quoting from the book of James: 'faith without works is dead' (James 2:26, NWT). That same verse is given in the ESV as: 'For as the body apart from the spirit is dead, so also faith apart from works is dead.' Is James contradicting Paul? How are we to understand what James is saying?

James is not saying that works saves a person, rather he is showing that saving faith shows itself in works. Works do not bring about salvation, but works are the fruit of salvation. A person cannot claim to have faith and bear no good fruit. That kind of faith is indeed dead. Rather, if a person has true saving faith, it will be shown in a changed life that seeks to live in obedience to Christ and his Word.

TIP:

Give a Jehovah's Witness the following hypothetical scenario. You have just been stabbed in the back and you only have three minutes to live. Seeing the Jehovah's Witnesses on the street, and knowing that they are religious people, you ask in desperation, 'What must I do to be saved?'

This is a difficult question for the Jehovah's Witnesses. In their mind, you don't have enough time. You need to 'exercise faith', which for them means to put on their 'Sunday best', attend meetings at the Kingdom Hall, knock on doors, get baptised as a Witness and be obedient to the Watch Tower. Therefore their answer to the question 'What must I do to be saved?' ranges from silence to 'It's up to Jehovah.'

In fact, the Watch Tower Society, through whom they believe Jehovah speaks, has already answered that question: '*Only Jehovah's Witnesses*, those of the anointed remnant and the "great crowd," as a united organization under the protection of the Supreme Organizer, *have any Scriptural hope of surviving* the impending end of this doomed system dominated by Satan the Devil.'[17] Elsewhere it has declared: 'Similarly, Jehovah is using *only one organization today* to accomplish his will. *To receive everlasting life* in the earthly Paradise we must identify that organization and serve God as part of it.'[18]

But for those Jehovah's Witnesses struggling to answer the question, I put pressure on them: 'I have only two minutes left'; 'I have only one minute left'. When they give no solid answer, I ask if they know what the biblical answer is to that question. They usually don't, so then I encourage them to read from their Bible Acts 16:28–31:

But Paul called out with a loud voice: 'Do not hurt yourself, for we are all here!' So he [the jailer] asked for lights and rushed in, and seized with trembling, he fell down before Paul and Silas. He brought them outside and said: 'Sirs, what must I do to get saved?' They said: 'Believe in the Lord Jesus, and you will get saved, you and your household' (NWT).

Even their Bible shows that the biblical answer to the question 'What must I do to be saved?' is 'Believe in the Lord Jesus, and you will get saved, you and your household.'

It is important to note that Jehovah's Witnesses have been taught that there will be a second chance for those who die before Armageddon. So if you have only three minutes to live, you will be resurrected to the paradise earth and given a further chance to 'exercise faith' in Jehovah during the millennial reign of Christ. But that means that they are basically teaching that, so long as you die before Armageddon, you can live how you want because you are guaranteed a second chance!

The Bible knows nothing of a second chance. In fact, it tells us: *'And just as it is appointed for man to die once, and after that comes judgment, so*

Christ, having been offered once to bear the sins of many, will appear a second time, not to deal with sin but to save those who are eagerly waiting for him (Hebrews 9:27–28).

QUESTIONS FOR JEHOVAH'S WITNESSES

Ask them to read John 6:47 in their Bible: 'Most truly I say to you, whoever believes has everlasting life' (NWT). Then ask them to read 1 John 5:12–13 in their Bible: 'The one who has the Son has this life; the one who does not have the Son of God does not have this life. I write you these things so that you may know that you have life everlasting, you who put your faith in the name of the Son of God' (NWT). Follow this with the questions:

- Do you have the Son?

- Do you *know* you have everlasting life?

- Do you have assurance that you have *been* saved?

CONTINUE ↓

Afterwards, ask them to read Luke 23:42–43. In these verses one of the criminals crucified beside Jesus says, 'Jesus, remember me when you come into your kingdom.' To this Jesus replies, 'Truly, I say to you, today you will be with me in Paradise.' Then ask the Jehovah's Witness exactly what the criminal had to do to be saved. The answer is to put his faith alone in Jesus' power to bring him into his kingdom.

10

HEAVEN AND THE 144,000

Jehovah's Witness teaching:
The Jehovah's Witnesses have a two-tier
salvation. They believe that only 144,000,
known as the 'anointed class', will reside
in heaven as priests and kings alongside
Jesus. They will reign over a 'great crowd'
on a paradise earth.

This Watch Tower doctrine comes from
Revelation 7:4 and its description of those
servants of God who are 'sealed'. It is interesting
to note that the Jehovah's Witnesses believe

the number 144,000 to be literal, but the tribes of Israel listed in the following verses to be spiritual (claiming themselves to be spiritual Israel). There is absolutely no justification for a literal *and* spiritual interpretation of these verses unless, of course, you are trying to make it fit a previously held theological view.

ESTABLISHING THE TRUE MEANING OF THE 144,000 IN REVELATION

Begin by asking Jehovah's Witnesses to read aloud from their Bible Revelation 6:12 to Revelation 7:16, pointing out that in the original manuscripts there were no chapters and verses. As they are reading, stop them when they get to the end of chapter 6 – verse 17 – and ask where this is taking place. The answer is clearly on the earth:

> … the stars of heaven fell to the *earth* as when a fig tree shaken by a high wind drops its unripe figs … every mountain and every island was removed from its place. Then the kings of the *earth*, the high officials, the military commanders, the rich, the strong, every slave, and every

free person *hid in the caves and among the rocks of the mountains* (Revelation 6:13–15, NWT, italics mine).

Ask them to continue reading aloud from Revelation 7:1–3 and then stop them once more, asking where this is taking place. Again, it is clearly on the earth:

After this I saw four angels standing on the four corners of the *earth*, holding tight the four winds of the *earth*, so that no wind could blow on the *earth* or on the sea or on any tree. And I saw another angel ascending from the sunrise, having a seal of the living God; and he called with a loud voice to the four angels to whom it was granted to harm the *earth* and the sea, saying: '*Do not harm the earth or the sea or the trees,* until after we have sealed the slaves of our God in their foreheads' (NWT, italics mine).

Then ask them to continue reading aloud from 7:4–8 before asking, 'Where are the 144,000?'

The context clearly shows the 144,000 are on the earth! They may well disagree, but persevere by having them read aloud from 7:9–16:

After this I saw, and look! a great crowd, which no man was able to number, out of all nations and tribes and peoples and tongues, *standing before the throne and before the Lamb, dressed in white robes;* and there were palm branches in their hands. And they keep shouting with a loud voice, saying: 'Salvation we owe to our God, who is seated on the throne, and to the Lamb.'

All the angels were *standing around the throne* and the elders and the four living creatures, and they *fell facedown before the throne* and worshipped God, saying: 'Amen! Let the praise and the glory and the wisdom and the thanksgiving and the honor and the power and the strength be to our God forever and ever. Amen.'

In response one of the elders said to me: 'These who are dressed in the white robes, who are they and where did they come from?' So right away I said to him: 'My lord, you are the one who knows.' And he said to me: 'These are the ones who come out of the great tribulation, and they have washed their robes and made them white in the blood of the Lamb. That is why they are *before the throne of God*, and they are rendering him sacred service day and night *in his temple;* and the One seated on the throne will spread his tent over them' (NWT, italics mine).

Ask them where all this is taking place. It is clearly happening in heaven.

In other words, these verses show the opposite of what the Jehovah's Witnesses have been taught. It is the 144,000 who are on the earth and it is the 'great crowd' who are in heaven.

QUESTIONS FOR JEHOVAH'S WITNESSES

When Jehovah's Witnesses repeatedly state that the 'great crowd' will be on the earth, ask them to read aloud

CONTINUE ↓

Revelation 19:1 from their Bible: 'After this I heard what seemed to be a loud voice of a great crowd in heaven. They said: "Praise Jah! The salvation and the glory and the power belong to our God"' (NWT). Then ask them where the great crowd will be according to this verse. You will be amazed by their answer: 'on the earth'. If you repeat all this, you will be doubly amazed that they again say: 'on the earth'.

Point out that they are now disagreeing with the Word of God. They may say that there is more than one great crowd, but this is not provable from Scripture. Alternatively they may state that this is a great crowd of angels, which again is not provable from Scripture.

Then follow up by enquiring why they deny what the Scripture clearly says. This demonstrates that they are blindly following the organisation and its theology, rather than the Bible.

11

THE RESURRECTION OF JESUS

Jehovah's Witness teaching:
Jehovah's Witnesses believe that Jesus rose
from the dead spiritually and not physically.

In denying the physical resurrection of Christ,
Jehovah's Witnesses put themselves at odds with
the Bible – and in serious danger. The Apostle
Paul clearly stated:

*Now I would remind you, brothers, of the
gospel I preached to you, which you received, in*

*which you stand, and by which you are being
saved, if you hold fast to the word I preached
to you—unless you believed in vain.*

*For I delivered to you as of first importance
what I also received: that Christ died for our
sins in accordance with the Scriptures, that
he was buried, that he was raised on the
third day in accordance with the Scriptures
(1 Corinthians 15:1–4).*

Therefore to deny the physical resurrection of
Jesus is to preach another gospel.

JESUS' DEATH

Jehovah's Witnesses believe that when Jesus
died, he no longer existed. They teach that
his body 'was disposed of by Jehovah God,
dissolved into its constituent elements or
atoms.'[19] So from the point of his death until
his resurrection, they say that Jesus – being only
a man – was completely gone.

This is consistent with what Jehovah's
Witnesses believe about all human beings.
They believe that humans do not have a

separate 'soul' or 'spirit', but that the soul or spirit refers to the person. Therefore, as humans are a soul, they believe death equals non-existence. Furthermore, they claim this is what the Bible teaches and quote Ecclesiastes 9:5 and 10 in support of it: 'For the living know that they will die, but the dead know nothing, and they have no more reward, because all memory of them is forgotten ... Whatever your hand finds to do, do with all your might, for there is no work nor planning nor knowledge nor wisdom in the Grave, where you are going' (NWT).

Their argument is quite easily answered by the context of Ecclesiastes. The constant refrain within the book is *'under the sun'*. The writer is speaking of all he sees around him in the world. When a person dies, he says they have no more involvement in all that happens 'under the sun'. But does the author mean there is no life beyond death? No, for he also says, *'... the dust returns to the earth as it was, and the spirit returns to God who gave it'* (Ecclesiastes 12:7).

JESUS' RESURRECTION

To prove Jesus' resurrection was only 'spiritual', Jehovah's Witnesses will next take you to a verse which, on first reading, appears to support their position: *'For Christ also suffered once for sins, the righteous for the unrighteous, that he might bring us to God, being put to death in the flesh but made alive in the spirit'* (1 Peter 3:18). Clearly, it's essential to understand the meaning of Jesus being 'made alive in the spirit'.

The Watch Tower teaches: 'God disposed of Jesus' body, not allowing it to see corruption and thus preventing its becoming a stumbling block to faith.'[20] Elsewhere it proclaims, 'Having given up his flesh for the life of the world, Christ could never take it again and become a man once more.'[21]

We can first consider what 'made alive in the spirit' cannot mean by allowing Scripture to interpret Scripture. Listen to what Jesus said:

I am the good shepherd. I know my own and my own know me, just as the Father knows me and I know the Father; and I lay down my life for the sheep. And I have other sheep that are not of this fold. I must bring them also, and they will listen to my voice. So there will be one flock, one shepherd. For this reason the Father loves me, because I lay down my life that I may take it up again. *No one takes it from me, but I lay it down of my own accord.* I have authority to lay it down, and I have authority to take it up again. *This charge I have received from my Father (John 10:14–18, emphasis mine).*

Is Jesus teaching here that his body would be disposed of? No! In fact, the Bible nowhere teaches that God would dispose of Jesus' body upon his death.

Elsewhere Jesus says:

So the Jews said to him, 'What sign do you show us for doing these things?' Jesus answered them, 'Destroy this temple, and in three days I will raise it up.' *The Jews then said, 'It has taken forty-six years to build this temple, and will you raise it up in three days?'* But he was speaking about the temple of his body. *When therefore he was raised from the dead, his disciples remembered that he had said this, and they believed the Scripture and the word that Jesus had spoken (John 2:18–22, emphasis mine).*

It is clear from the lips of Jesus that he would be resurrected in his body, that is physically resurrected. Jesus being *'made alive in the spirit'* cannot mean him being raised spiritually. So what does it mean? The NKJV translates it: *'made alive by the spirit'* (emphasis mine). The KJV translates it as *'quickened by the Spirit'*. Some translations have 'spirit' and others 'Spirit'. Believing that Jesus was raised by the Holy Spirit is certainly consistent with other verses in Scripture (such as Romans 1:4; 8:11). Though there are differences of opinion, I am happy to settle with this.

QUESTIONS FOR JEHOVAH'S WITNESSES

Ask Jehovah's Witnesses to read Matthew 10:28 in their Bible: 'And do not become fearful of those who kill the body but cannot kill the soul' (NWT). Jesus

CONTINUE ➡

believed in a separation of body and soul, so ask them if we shouldn't too.

Then take them to Luke 23:43 in their Bibles, where Jesus said to the criminal on the cross: 'Truly I tell you today, you will be with me in Paradise' (NWT). Now ask how both Jesus and the criminal can be in paradise that day if death equals non-existence. (Note, please be aware that the New World Translation moves the comma to after the word 'today', thus making it look like Jesus was saying he was making his statement that day, not promising paradise that day. But why did he need to tell the criminal that he was making his statement that day? Wasn't that obvious?)

Next, ask Jehovah's Witnesses to read and explain their understanding of John 2:19: *'Destroy this temple, and in three days I will raise it up.'* Jesus is claiming that he will raise himself. He can only do that if he is God. Another unambiguous Scripture to share with the Jehovah's Witnesses to prove

CONTINUE ↓

Jesus was not raised as a 'spirit creature' is Luke 24:36–39:

As they were talking about these things, Jesus himself stood among them, and said to them, 'Peace to you!' But they were startled and frightened and thought they saw a spirit. *And he said to them, 'Why are you troubled, and why do doubts arise in your hearts? See* my hands and my feet, that it is I myself. Touch me, and see. For a spirit does not have flesh and bones as you see that I have" *(emphasis mine).*

12

THE NEW WORLD TRANSLATION

The Bible used by Jehovah's Witnesses is called the New World Translation of the Holy Scriptures (NWT). They claim that the NWT is the most accurate Bible available, having been produced by scholars trained in biblical languages.

In 2013, the latest revision of the NWT was released amidst great excitement from the faithful. This is what the foreword to this 'new' NWT says:

Recognizing the importance of the Bible's message, we have undertaken the revision of this text with a profound respect for the content of the Bible. *We feel the full weight of our responsibility to convey its message accurately.* This revised edition has built on the fine foundation laid in previous editions of the New World Translation of the Holy Scriptures, a Bible that was first released more than 60 years ago. However, the English language has changed during the past half century. Such change prompted current members of the *New World Bible Translation Committee* to initiate this comprehensive revision. Our goal has been to produce a translation that is not only faithful to the original texts but also clear and easy to read. The Appendix articles 'Principles of Bible Translation,' 'Features of This Revision,' and 'How the Bible Came to Us' discuss *some of the linguistic refinements* that were made in this edition (italics mine).

Let us consider some of the claims made by this foreword.

1.THE NWT WILL 'CONVEY ITS MESSAGE ACCURATELY' WITH 'SOME ... LINGUISTIC REFINEMENTS'

How accurate is the NWT? You would be hard pushed to find any reputable expert in biblical languages who endorses this translation.

TIP:

Don't be fooled when the Watch Tower quotes 'scholars' in their literature who appear to support the NWT. You should check out the scholar's credentials, for example whether their area of expertise is biblical languages.

It is not possible within the scope of this book to list every questionable change within the NWT, but let me point out some significant ones, some of which have been mentioned already:

- The addition of the word 'other' in Colossians 1:15–20 to obscure Jesus' divinity.

- The removal of the prefix 'the' before the Holy Spirit, thus designating him impersonal. Also, the replacement of the Holy Spirit with an unbiblical 'active force' (which sounds more like *Star Wars!*). This is seen, for example, in: 'In the beginning God created the heavens and the earth. Now the earth was formless and desolate, and there was darkness upon the surface of the watery deep, and *God's active force* was moving about over the surface of the waters' (Genesis 1:1–2, NWT, my italics).

- The addition of the words 'union with' to describe believers' relationship with Jesus because they do not accept Christ can be 'in you'. We see this, for example, in: '… to whom God has been pleased to make known among the nations the glorious riches of this sacred secret, which is Christ in union with you, the hope of his glory' (Colossians 1:27, NWT).

- The addition of the name Jehovah throughout the New Testament. This is totally unjustified because it is nowhere found in the Greek.

- The removal of the word 'worship' (which is changed to 'obeisance') whenever it is used in relation to Jesus. For example, Matthew 28:16–18 in the New World Translation reads: 'However, the 11 disciples went to Gal'i·lee to the mountain where Jesus had arranged for them to meet. When they saw him, they did *obeisance*, but some doubted. Jesus approached and spoke to them, saying: "All authority has been given me in heaven and on the earth"' (italics mine). This change is also inconsistent because in every other occurrence (apart from when it is used in a general sense and once towards the Apostle Peter), the Greek word *proskuneo* is translated 'worship' in the NWT.

- Similarly, they correctly translate the Greek *ego eimi* as 'I am' everywhere in the NWT except in John 8:58 because they cannot accept Jesus claiming to be the God of the Old Testament. Therefore, they translate this verse: 'Jesus said to them: "Most truly I say to you, before Abraham came into existence, *I have been*"' (NWT, italics mine).

Compare this with the ESV: *'Jesus said to them, "Truly, truly, I say to you, before Abraham was, I am."'* The Watch Tower's problem with Jesus saying, 'I am' stems from the fact that by it Jesus is declaring his divinity. In Exodus 3:14, we see God use the same expression: *'God said to Moses, "I AM WHO I AM." And he said, "Say this to the people of Israel, 'The LORD ... has sent me to you.'"'* Therefore, they also have modified their translation of that verse to: 'So God said to Moses: "I Will Become What I Choose to Become." And he added: "This is what you are to say to the Israelites, 'I Will Become has sent me to you'"' (NWT). But when Jesus said; 'before Abraham was, I am', the Jews clearly knew that he was claiming to be divine because of their response: *'So they picked up stones to throw at him, but Jesus hid himself and went out of the temple'* (John 8:59). Surely the reaction of his Jewish hearers is disproportionate if Jesus is only claiming to have lived before Abraham. Furthermore, they could only stone him for blasphemy, so what else could they have understood him to be saying?

- The addition of an 'a' to the text of John 1:1 to make Jesus only 'a god', and not the God. Therefore, their translation of that verse reads: 'In the beginning was the Word, and the Word was with God, and the Word was *a god*' (NWT, my italics). In contrast the ESV, along with most Bible translations, states, 'the Word was God.' Yet if Jesus is only 'a god', why in their Bibles does Thomas call him, 'My Lord and my God!' (John 20:28, NWT)?

All in all, these are gross mistranslations of God's Word. The NWT purposely seeks to hide the deity of Christ from its readers. At other times Jehovah's Witnesses will try to bamboozle you with reference to the original Greek, but they are rarely proficient in Greek and are merely repeating what they have been told.

2. THE EXISTENCE OF THE NEW WORLD BIBLE TRANSLATION COMMITTEE

The second point to address is who are the people responsible for the NWT? This is a good question to ask the Jehovah's Witnesses. Their usual response is to say that the committee members wish to remain anonymous so that no glory goes to them. In reality, this is a shrewd move as, if their names were revealed, their credentials could be checked, and it may be discovered that they had no biblical linguistic or translation skills whatsoever.

TIP:

Ask Jehovah's Witnesses if they would allow you to perform an operation on them. If they say no, ask them why. They should say something along the lines of wanting to know you are properly qualified and that they can trust you. If, on the other hand, they say yes, question whether they would want to know for sure beforehand that you are trained to do so. From this, you can ask why they trust their Bible translation when they don't know the names or qualifications of its translators. Continue by explaining that you can obtain the names and credentials of the people who translated your Bible. Indeed, the Bible writers themselves had no problem

CONTINUE ➡

adding their name to their letters. Nor does knowing the names of Bible authors such as Paul and Peter cause a person to worship them or give them glory.

QUESTIONS FOR JEHOVAH'S WITNESSES

- If I told you I was a Greek scholar and can translate the Bible, would you believe me? I may be able to impress you with speaking a few Greek words, but I could be lying about my ability to translate. So, what evidence would you accept as proof that I am telling the truth?

- Would it be good to just accept that a person is telling you the truth without checking their credentials? Suppose you wanted an extension on your house. Would you trust someone to do that without any evidence that he is a qualified builder?

- In the same way, why would you trust those who claim to be qualified to

CONTINUE ↓

translate your Bible, but who remain anonymous. If your Bible has been changed or had things added/taken away, this is incredibly serious and can affect your eternal future.

13

HOW DO WE REACH JEHOVAH'S WITNESSES WITH THE GOSPEL?

Asking Jehovah's Witnesses questions, discussing Bible verses with them and sharing your testimony and how God answers your prayers are all good ways of engaging with them. The Holy Spirit can work through all these means to help a Jehovah's Witness to wake up spiritually. However, I have found we usually need to use CPR.

C = CARE – SHARING THE TRUTH IN LOVE

…but in your hearts regard Christ the Lord as holy, always being prepared to make a defence to anyone who asks you for a reason for the hope that is in you; yet do it with gentleness and respect, having a good conscience, so that, when you are slandered, those who revile your good behaviour in Christ may be put to shame (1 Peter 3:15–16).

It is vitally important that we care for Jehovah's Witnesses. They need to see that we love them. Sharing the gospel with them is not about showing yourself right and them wrong. How can we show that we *really* care about them?

When they get you out of bed at a silly hour on a Saturday morning to answer their knock on your door, smile at them. Tell them it is good to see them and share with them how you love the Bible.

Unless you have thoroughly memorised this book, you will probably not be ready then for an in-depth discussion on the Trinity, but you have some other choices:

- You could invite them back at a more convenient time. Note, though, that inviting them into your home can be extremely dangerous because the enemy has shipwrecked many a churchgoer's faith through this group. Some believers may argue that 2 John 9–10 prohibits us from having cult members in our houses, though this would not be my understanding of those verses. As a rule, though, do not invite them in if you are not sure exactly what you believe and, more importantly, why you believe it. If you want to meet with them, you could invite a mature Christian to join you. I tend to meet them on neutral ground, such as at a coffee house or the like.

- When you meet Jehovah's Witnesses for the first time, they may suggest you go through one of their publications. It is okay to do that and to ask questions along the way. Remember they like to be the teacher and you must appear to be the student. The first few meetings are all about making a friendship with them. As you progress, you can then ask more difficult questions and even challenge them. They will be more likely to answer and engage with you once you have become friends by showing them love and care.

- Sharing your testimony is powerful. Tell the Jehovah's Witness how you came to have a relationship with God, how you know that your sins are forgiven because Jesus died for you, and that your future is secure because Jesus rose back to life. You have what they are searching for, so do not keep it to yourself.

TIP:

Heed Paul's advice to the church at Ephesus. We are involved in a battle for souls, so we must put on the full armour of God:

Finally, be strong in the Lord and in the strength of his might. Put on the whole armour of God, that you may be able to stand against the schemes of the devil. For we do not wrestle against flesh and blood, but against the rulers,

CONTINUE ➡

> *against the authorities, against the cosmic powers over this present darkness, against the spiritual forces of evil in the heavenly places. Therefore, take up the whole armour of God, that you may be able to withstand in the evil day, and having done all, to stand firm. Stand therefore, having fastened on the belt of truth, and having put on the breastplate of righteousness, and, as shoes for your feet, having put on the readiness given by the gospel of peace. In all circumstances take up the shield of faith, with which you can extinguish all the flaming darts of the evil one; and take the helmet of salvation, and the sword of the Spirit, which is the word of God, praying at all times in the Spirit, with all prayer and supplication' (Ephesians 6:10–18).*

P = PRAYER – BATTLING IN THE HEAVENLIES FOR THE SOULS OF THE LOST

Prayer is the real key to their freedom. We are engaging in spiritual warfare when we enter into a discussion with a cult member: *'For we do not wrestle against flesh and blood, but against the rulers, against the authorities, against the cosmic powers over this present darkness, against the spiritual forces of evil in the heavenly places'* (Ephesians 6:12). We must be aware that the people on our doorstep are not the issue, rather it is the enemy who has blinded them: *'In their case the god of this world has blinded the minds of the unbelievers, to keep them from seeing the light of the gospel of the glory of Christ, who is the image of God'* (2 Corinthians 4:4).

Rather like Saul before he was converted – and became Paul – cult members *'have a zeal for God, but not according to knowledge'* (Romans 10:2). They need to have the scales taken from their eyes, something which only the Spirit of God can do. So pray that God would open their eyes and their hearts. Ask the Holy Spirit to reveal to them who the Lord Jesus truly is. Once you know some of their names, set up a prayer group or ask your church to pray for them.

R = RESOLVE

Friends, be encouraged that people are 'waking up' and leaving cults. After many encounters with Jehovah's Witnesses, you may feel you have been banging your head against a brick wall and your efforts have been a waste of time. But don't let the enemy plague you with such thoughts. We are to sow seeds and pray, leaving the results of our efforts in the hands of our merciful God. So, resolve to keep going, keep sharing, keep loving.

Ask God to give you such a burden for the Jehovah's Witnesses that you may be used to reach these lost people for Christ.

Lord, help us to bear fruit in this forgotten mission field.

14

HOW CAN WE HELP THOSE LEAVING THE JEHOVAH'S WITNESSES?

Leaving a cult is incredibly costly. Those who leave the Jehovah's Witnesses are told they are leaving God. They may well also be leaving behind family, friends, work and everything they have ever known.

Many who decide to leave the Jehovah's Witnesses can therefore quickly find themselves very lost and lonely in a confusing world – a world they had previously been separate from as they believed it was evil. They suddenly must think for themselves and can struggle with everyday living. Whilst they have chosen to leave the cult, the cult doesn't quickly leave them, such is the psychological hold that these groups have over their adherents. As a result, those who have left the Jehovah's Witnesses will be anxious, wondering if they have made the correct decision in leaving. The church can also be a scary place to those who have been constantly told that churches are 'pagan' and 'of the devil'.

PRACTICAL TIPS

Before I left the Jehovah's Witnesses, a Christian helped me. He was kind and patient towards me. He had his church praying for me from the moment he met me! I have already mentioned the importance of prayer and we must pray for those seeking to leave the group. But they will also need practical help in the following ways:

- They will need friendship as they will most likely have been shunned by their family and friends still in the Jehovah's Witnesses.

- They will need practical support, as they may struggle to live outside of the organisation.

- They will need patience, as they will still believe some of the things they have been taught and be confused about Christian belief and practice.

- They will need love, as they have lost all that they once held dear.

Without support from loving, compassionate Christian believers, the struggling Jehovah's Witness may well head back to the organisation. Alternatively, they may drift into atheism, rejecting everything to do with religion. May we with love and patience, point them to the one who can truly heal them and set them free.

RECOMMENDED RESOURCES

James R. White, *The Forgotten Trinity: Rediscovering the Heart of the Christian Faith* (Bethany House Publishers, 1998).

Ron Rhodes, *Reasoning from the Scriptures with the Jehovah's Witnesses* (Harvest House Publishers, updated and expanded edition 2009).

Don Cameron, *Captives of a Concept: Understanding the Illusionary Concept that Holds Millions of Jehovah's Witnesses Captive* (Lulu.com, 2005).

Doug Harris, *Awake! To the Watchtower* (Reachout Trust, 2006).

To hear my testimony, go online:
www.cults-investigated.com

NOTES

1. *The Watchtower*, 1 September 1989, p. 19 (italics mine).

2. *The Watchtower*, 15 February 1981, pp. 16–19.

3. *The Watchtower*, 15 February 1983, p. 12 (italics mine).

4. Their belief is that those outside of the Jehovah's Witnesses who die before Armageddon will be resurrected back to life on the paradise earth and given a second chance to be obedient to Jehovah.

5. Don Cameron, *Captives of a Concept: Anatomy of an Illusion* (Lulu.com, 2005), p. 12.

6. https://www.jwfacts.com/watchtower/1975.php

7. *The Watchtower*, 15 March 1980, p. 17.

8. *Aid to Bible Understanding* (Watch Tower, 1971), p. 885.

9. *What Does the Bible Really Teach?* (Watch Tower, 2006), p. 41.

10. 'What Is the Holy Spirit?', JW.org: https://www.jw.org/en/bible-teachings/questions/what-is-the-holy-spirit/

11. 'Is God a Trinity?', JW.org: https://www.jw.org/en/bible-teachings/questions/trinity

12. *New Catholic Encyclopedia* (1967), Volume 14, p. 299.

13. *Encyclopædia Britannica* (1970), Volume 6, p. 386, as quoted in 'Myth 4: God Is a Trinity' JW.org: https://www.jw.org/en/publications/magazines/wp20091101/myth-god-is-a-trinity

14. 'What is Salvation?', JW.org: https://www.jw.org/en/bible-teachings/questions/what-is-salvation

15. *The Watchtower*, 1 July 1984, p. 6 (emphasis mine).

16. *Watchtower*, 15 January 1986, p. 101 (emphasis mine).

17. *The Watchtower*, 1 September 1989, p. 19 (italics mine).

18. *The Watchtower*, 15 February 1983, p. 12 (italics mine).

19. *The Watchtower*, 1 September 1953, p. 518.

20. *The Watchtower*, 15 November 1991, p. 31.

21. *You Can Live Forever in Paradise on Earth* (Watch Tower, 1982), p. 143.

a division of **10**ofthose.com

10Publishing is the publishing house of **10ofThose**.
It is committed to producing quality Christian
resources that are biblical and accessible.

www.10ofthose.com is our online retail arm selling
thousands of quality books at discounted prices.

For information contact: **info@10ofthose.com**
or check out our website: **www.10ofthose.com**